SURVIVING THE TRIALS

Kenny Dietrich

Surviving the Trials

Kenny Dietrich

Copyright @ 2017 UglyTent, LLC

Second Edition 2020

Print ISBN: 978-0-9995792-0-6

e-Book ISBN: 978-0-9995792-1-3

Unless otherwise noted, all scriptures are taken from the THE HOLY BIBLE, ENGLISH STANDARD VERSION (ESV): Scriptures taken from THE HOLY BIBLE, ENGLISH STANDARD VERSION ® Copyright© 2001 by Crossway, a publishing ministry of Good News Publishers.

Cover art by Will Gossage.

All rights reserved. This book is protected by copyright. No part of this book may be reproduced or transmitted in any form or by any means, electronic or mechanical, including photocopying, recording, or by any information storage and retrieval system, without permission in writing from the publisher.

The purpose of this book is to educate and enlighten. This book is sold with the understanding that the author and publisher are not engaged in rendering counseling, albeit it professional or lay, to the reader or anyone else. The author and publisher shall have neither liability nor responsibility to any person or entity with respect to any loss or damage caused, or alleged to have been caused, directly or indirectly, by the information contained in this book.

Dedicated to my father, Harry Dietrich

Cover Art by Will Gossage

Contents

PREFACE 1
1 LIGHTEN YOUR LOAD 5
2 MY FATHER 13
3 SUFFERING 21
4 TYLER 30
5 HOPE 39
6 THE LORD'S WILL 55
7 MORE TRIALS AHEAD 71
8 GOD'S PEOPLE STEP UP 85
9 FRIENDSHIP 95
10 YOU ARE NOT ALONE 101
11 HEALING 115
12 GOD WILL NOT PUT MORE ON YOU THAN YOU CAN HANDLE 121
EPILOGUE 129
ABOUT THE AUTHOR 131

Surviving the Trials by Kenny Dietrich

PREFACE

You won't believe some of the things I've seen. From the heart-wrenching to the miraculous and the truly unbelievable, yet uplifting. These are my firsthand accounts of God working in my life. This book will shock, amaze, encourage, and hopefully inspire.

Not that I'm great—it's just that the things that have happened to me are great. God has done so much for me, and I want to share some of these stories and testimonies with you. I have opened myself up and poured my heart into these pages.

So many times, we lose the stories of our loved ones as they are forgotten over time or lost with the ones gone on before us. I wanted to take my stories and put them in writing, both to glorify God and to keep them around for generations to come.

My dad lived his life overcoming adversity. Being a Russian refugee, he fought both language and cultural barriers as a child and he suffered from severe health issues as an adult. But that didn't stop him from having a wonderful life.

My son Tyler's story is just as incredible as my father's. Tyler has faced adversity with health issues more than half of his life. His childhood was stolen from him by pediatric cancer. Although he is now a cancer survivor, he still suffers from the "late effects" of his illness.

Tragedy struck our family and changed my perspective once again with the untimely passing of my father-in-law. Jim was an amazing person, the likes of whom I've never met before.

Surviving the Trials by Kenny Dietrich

All of these trials have made me who I am today. A *trial* is a trail that can lead you to a better spiritual life. I am a better person and a stronger Christian because of them. Please continue to turn the pages to read about my journey, and I pray that you will receive a blessing from my labors.

Surviving the Trials by Kenny Dietrich

Surviving the Trials by Kenny Dietrich

1
LIGHTEN YOUR LOAD

I love being in the wilderness. It is there that I feel the closest to God. I find the woods to be beautiful no matter what the season, just as I've learned to find beauty in my life, no matter what season I'm experiencing.

I spend a lot of time in the forest, and I'm just as comfortable there as I am in my own house. I am captivated by the strength of the trees and the beauty of their leaves. I have fallen in love with the smells of the wilderness, and I often find myself standing completely still with my eyes closed, taking in the fragrances. The sounds are just as incredible, but you must be willing to listen in order to hear some of the ones that are hidden.

Surviving the Trials by Kenny Dietrich

The wilderness is a great teacher, and some of my experiences have not been as pleasurable as others. But I have learned even to enjoy the inclement weather, although overpacking in that situation can be a problem. As far as amenities goes, I can make myself extremely comfortable in the wilderness with very little. The more I know, and the more I've learned, the less I carry with me when I leave my home.

Imagine being in the woods carrying everything you're going to need for the next few days on your back. It's just you, all by yourself. Take a moment to think about this question: What you will need? What would you put in your backpack?

Would you want to carry a twenty-five-pound four-person tent that you bought at your local box store, or would you rather carry a one-man backpacking tent that

Surviving the Trials by Kenny Dietrich

weighs just three pounds and can be compacted into the size of a two-liter bottle? How about a sleeping bag? Would you like a ten-pound flannel bag the size of a small child, or a lightweight down bag that can be stuffed into a sack the size of a football? What about food and water? A gallon of water weighs just over eight pounds, and the average person needs to drink a half gallon each day. What else do you need in your journey? How many creature comforts could you do without?

These comparisons are to make a point the best way I know how. I compare much of my life's journey to my wanderings in the outdoors. If we wouldn't carry any extra weight into the wilderness and unnecessarily burden ourselves there, why then, in life, do we carry unnecessary mental, emotional, and spiritual baggage? Just as with my backpacking and camping in the wilderness, the same principle applies to my walk in and through this life. I do not want to carry extra weight. I don't want to carry the heavy burden of worry, unforgiveness, or sin.

The Bible tells us in Proverbs 12:25: "*Anxiety in a man's heart weighs him down, but a good word makes him glad.*" Numerous times the Word of God tells us to cast our worries on Him, because He cares for us. He can handle our burdens.

In the parable of the unforgiving servant, Jesus clearly explained the importance of forgiveness and how our heavenly Father views it. He compared the kingdom of heaven to a king who wished to settle accounts with his servants. When the king began to do this, a servant who owed him 10,000 talents was brought before him. The king ordered him to be sold, his wife to be sold, and even for his children to be sold in order to pay the debt. The servant fell to his knees and pleaded with his king. But once the king had forgiven the servant, the servant immediately went to someone who owed *him* and demanded that payment be made. When that person couldn't pay up, the servant who had just been forgiven placed the man who owed him the debt in prison. When the king got word of this, he summoned the servant and said to him:

> *"You wicked servant! I forgave you all that debt because you pleaded with me. And should not you have had mercy on your fellow servant, as I had mercy on you?" And in anger his master delivered him to the jailers, until he should pay all his debt. So also my heavenly Father will do*

to every one of you, if you do not forgive your brother from your heart.

—Matthew 18:32–35

We should be taking the same amount of forgiveness that Jesus gave to us and we should be giving that amount to someone else. We are not called to hold on to anger and bitterness; we are not animals of burden. We were not created to carry the weight of unforgiveness.

First John 1:9 tells us: "*If we confess our sins, he is faithful and just to forgive us our sins and to cleanse us from all unrighteousness.*" When we are forgiven from our sins, we are to take heart in knowing that we are washed clean of all of our transgressions. Jesus paid the price for our sins on the cross. There is no need to carry the heavy burden of sin any longer.

Surviving the Trials by Kenny Dietrich

Matthew 11:28–30 tell us: *"Come to me, all who labor and are heavy laden, and I will give you rest. Take my yoke upon you, and learn from me, for I am gentle and lowly in heart, and you will find rest for your souls. For my yoke is easy, and my burden is light."* Exchange your heavy burden for the light one that Jesus has for you.

Surviving the Trials by Kenny Dietrich

2
MY FATHER

When I was a young man just starting out on my own, I rented an apartment in a complex with three other units. One beautiful summer day, I washed my pickup truck inside and out. After I finished, I popped the hood and started to clean the engine and check the fluids. I'll be honest, this was about all I knew to do under the hood.

One of the other apartment renters, a young man about my age, walked over to the truck and asked me what I was working on. I tried to play it cool, acting like I knew exactly what I was doing. I said, "I'm just checking the fluids and cleaning the engine up a bit." Obviously, he could tell I didn't have a clue what I was doing, and he went on to explain the engine and all of its components to me. After about twenty minutes of this, I asked him how he knew so much about cars. He said that he gained his knowledge from his dad, who was really good with engines.

A different conversation ensued as we talked about our fathers. Come to find out, his dad wasn't around, having left him and his mom at a very crucial time in his life, never to be seen again.

As the young man walked away, I felt cheated because my dad hadn't taught me the finer points of auto mechanics. But then it occurred to me that what my dad taught me was a lot more important. Dad taught me how to be a good Christian man, husband, and father, and how to show love to others.

Surviving the Trials by Kenny Dietrich

I am the first generation on my father's side to born in the United States. I am the son of an immigrant, and I am proud of it. Dad used to tell the story of coming to America, seeing Lady Liberty walking on Ellis Island, the whole nine yards. The people at the immigration office offered my grandmother a job as a translator because she spoke five different languages: German, Russian, Ukrainian, Polish, and English. However, she refused the job, still worried that the Russians might find her and take her back to her homeland.

Four generations before my grandmother had been born in the Ukraine, our family lived in Germany. We migrated to the Ukraine when it was still part of Russia for a better life. Russia was trying to build itself into a great and powerful nation at that time, and it was looking for good people with both skills and drive to come to their country and work. My family had some trade skills and saw an opportunity to better themselves.

Like all strong families, they kept in touch the best they could with each other, only to find themselves considered to be traitors later on during World War II. The Russians traced our communications with our German relatives, simple family discussions, and considered it treason.

After they shot and killed my great-great-grandfather and another relative, our family fled back to Germany. My grandmother Louise, my grandfather Rhinehart, and their infant son (my father, Harry—pronounced Harrie) literally fled on foot under gunfire and aerial attacks back to Germany.

Eventually seeking revenge, my grandfather, along with others in our family, joined the German army to strike back at the Russians. It is there that Rhinehart's story ends. He was captured and died as a prisoner of war at a camp in Siberia.

My grandmother Louise, my father, Harry, and the newest addition to the family, his younger sister, Gertrude, lived in Germany until the war was over. They eventually found sponsorship and a way to the United States, the land of the free.

That may be why Dad and his family members always seemed to have a better understanding of what this country truly stands for: the freedom, the liberties, the opportunities, and the melting pot of humanity. Dad was not one to take things for granted.

I realize that not everyone is blessed with a good father, or even a father at all. My heart aches for people who have not had that blessing. However, we all have a heavenly Father, and He wants you to know Him and have a relationship with Him.

He already knows you, better then you know yourself, and He loves you like no one else ever will. Luke 12:7 tells us, "*Why, even the hairs of your head are all numbered.*"

Jesus explained how we should talk daily to God, our heavenly Father, in detail in Matthew 6:9: "*Our Father in heaven, hallowed be your name.*" Again, in Mark 14:36, when Jesus prayed in Gethsemane, "*Abba, Father, all things are possible for you,*" He could have said anything and used any combination of adjectives or proper titles such as "Mighty King," "Powerful Lord," or "Creator of the Universe." But He didn't. He wants us to talk to God as we would talk to our earthly fathers.

Why is this so important? Because it establishes a truly personal relationship with our Lord and Savior, Jesus Christ, and with our heavenly Father. In 1 John 3:1, John wrote: "*See what kind of love the Father has given to us, that we should be called children of God.*" He went on to say that having a relationship with the Father and the Son will tremendously change our daily lives (see verses 4–10).

Like our earthly fathers, He wants what is best for us. Jeremiah 29:11 says: "*For I know the plans I have for you, declares the Lord, plans for welfare and not for evil, to give you a future and a hope.*"

Sometimes He allows us to stumble and fall, but He helps to pick us back up again. Psalm 37:23–24 states, "*The steps of a man are established by the Lord, when he delights in his way; though he fall, he shall not be cast headlong, for the* LORD *upholds his hand."*

We are never truly alone. Our heavenly Father walks with us. Sometimes He is by our side, sometimes He is ahead, and, as the poem goes, sometimes He carries us.

3
SUFFERING

My dad hadn't spoken in three hours. He lay in his bed resting in a morphine-induced sleep. His breathing was slow and heavy, but we were all glad he had settled down. Hospice had told us that the end was near, so the family gathered at Mom and Dad's house out in the country.

I had visited Dad a few days before, and I knew he wasn't doing well. The evening of my visit, Mom asked me if I wanted to wake him from his nap and I did. I helped him out of bed and into his robe. Always the gentleman, Dad believed a housecoat or a robe was necessary attire when not in bed or fully dressed. I walked him to the bathroom and even had to help him get seated on the toilet. After this, he wanted to comb his hair and brush his teeth. I let Dad do as much as he could by himself, but when it came time to brush his teeth he reached for the toothpaste and started to squeeze some out onto the comb in his hand. Of course, I stopped him and replaced it with a toothbrush. That's when I realized just how bad things had become. He was declining fast.

My brother, Chris, along with his family, met us at Mom and Dad's house, and we settled in for what was to be a very long night. I was blessed to be able to say so many good-byes and to hold my sweet father as much as I wanted to that night. Saying good-bye to someone you love is never easy, but that night helped ease his passing. I know the Lord set it up that way for me and our family, and I recognize it as a gift that I'll always cherish.

In order to receive that gift, though, we first had to endure the suffering—both Dad's and our own. Suffering is humbling, and in this suffering, you give yourself over to God. Sometimes God allows us to go through a trial to humble us, because worry is actually a form of pride. Take comfort in knowing that suffering isn't meant to last forever. But also be cognizant of the Lord's timing, His proper timing.

Christians need not fear suffering. God has given us everything we need to get through it. Matthew 6:26 tells us that our heavenly Father takes care of the birds of the air: *"They neither sow nor reap nor gather into barns, and yet your heavenly Father feeds them."*

My earthly father was a fine example of a man who loved being outdoors, loved the wilderness, and loved all the animals in it, especially the winged creatures of the air. I heard him refer to Matthew 6:26 many times, but I didn't truly understand it until later in life. Dad rarely complained; he was a very content man. With my mother, Sue, as his companion, he had a great life. They were good to each other the way a husband and a wife are supposed to be. Mom and Dad gave my brother and me a great childhood filled with lots of wonderful memories, and for that I am forever thankful.

Dad always said he was glad he was the one who became sick, because he just couldn't take seeing any of us suffer. I told him many times that I was sorry he had always had such bad health, and he always replied, "Don't be, I'll be okay."

Surviving the Trials by Kenny Dietrich

I've heard many other people over the years say that they never knew Harry was sick, because he just never complained about it. He was always ready with a smile or a wave and sometimes a hug. One friend described it best when he said that Harry had an "infectious laugh." Get Dad laughing, and it was hard to get him to stop, and before long the entire room would be laughing with him.

On the night of his passing, he lay sleeping in his own bed, in his own home, surrounded by his family. My mother, my brother, all the grandchildren, even his beloved mother, Louise, were there, all of us by his bedside.

He hadn't spoken or moved in hours, and to tell the truth, I thought he would pass at any moment. Then suddenly he went into a coughing fit. Chris and I raised him up in bed to try to give him some relief. He coughed and sputtered, then started to breathe a little better. My heart was breaking as I watched him endure this awful death.

My eyes filled with tears, I said, "Dad, I am so sorry!" I was not expecting a response, nor was anyone else. But Dad opened his eyes briefly and looked in my direction. "Don't be," he replied with what was left of his strength. One last time he wanted to remind us that he was glad it was himself who was sick and not one of us.

That was the last thing I remember my father ever saying. It made me sad and I cried, but it also showed me how much he loved each of us all the way to the end of his life.

Surviving the Trials by Kenny Dietrich

First Peter 5:6–9 tell us: *"Humble yourselves, therefore, under the mighty hand of God so that at the proper time he may exalt you, casting all your anxieties on him, because he cares for you. Be sober-minded; be watchful. Your adversary the devil prowls around like a roaring lion, seeking someone to devour. Resist him, firm in your faith, knowing that the same kinds of suffering are being experienced by your brotherhood throughout the world."*

I love the visuals given to us in this passage of scripture. To me it is telling us to bow down, O great warrior, before your king. At the proper time, when your fight is finished, he will reward you. Once again, because you are strong in the faith, you have pushed back the enemy, the evil beast lurking in your lands. Your fellow warriors have done the same in their own lands, all in the unified mission to protect and further God's holy kingdom.

Just as Dad's fight was done, he received his reward, walking with Jesus in the land beyond this life. He had had a great visitation and funeral service; it was truly a celebration of his life. During the funeral, Pastor Jim gave the analogy of Dad standing on the shoreline, waiting for a ship to take him to the new lands of heaven. As he got on board the ship, we were still standing on the shore saying, "There he goes!" As he made his way from this life to the next, the people on the shores of heaven were saying, "Here he comes!"

First Peter 5:10 says: *"And after you have suffered a little while, the God of all grace, who has called you to his eternal glory in Christ, will himself restore, confirm, strengthen, and establish you."*

Surviving the Trials by Kenny Dietrich

4
TYLER

When I met Tyler, he was five months old. I had dated his mother, Heather, years before and hadn't seen her since. Tyler's biological father wasn't a good dad and he wasn't in the picture much. He was in and out of trouble, and in jail frequently. This caused many difficult situations when I was dating Tyler's mother. This was the first time I'd even been in the courthouse for anything other than renewing my driver's license. Eventually Tyler's dad was sent to prison for rape, and there he stayed to serve out the maximum sentence. After Heather and I were married, we eventually had another child, a beautiful baby girl named Madison.

Surviving the Trials by Kenny Dietrich

More than anything else, I loved being a father. Raising those two wonderful kids was my life. Be sure to enjoy yours when they're young—because they grow up fast!

When Tyler was six years old, I adopted him. He knew about his biological father and what a bad person he was, and so he looked at me as the only "dad" he'd really ever had.

In the middle of his kindergarten year, Tyler got himself into some trouble. I was working in an office when I got a phone call at my desk. It was the principal of the elementary school. My first response was to wonder, *What has Tyler done now?* His principal, who happened also to be my principal when I was a child, said that he had pulled the fire alarm. I told the principal that I'd be right there.

Surviving the Trials by Kenny Dietrich

When I arrived at the school, Tyler and the principal were waiting on me. Tyler looked up at me with big, sad eyes and said, "I tried to put it back." His principal smiled and placed his hand over his mouth, trying to suppress a laugh.

When I asked Tyler what happened, he explained that while he was standing in line, he looked up and read the words on the little red box on the wall. He explained, "The box said *P-U-L-L*, Daddy. That means to pull. So I pulled it."

Needless to say, Tyler wasn't in trouble very long, and his mistake was forgiven quickly. He was always extremely smart and perceptive. He has taught me so much about life, and I hope I have been able to teach him half as much as his father.

Children make great teachers. We can learn so much from them if we only open our eyes to see. I think sometimes we get too caught up in micromanaging their behavior that we miss the point of helping guide their ways.

Children watch us a lot more than we realize. Because of this, I have learned to do my best with them, every chance I get. I set an example, if you will.

One beautiful afternoon, Tyler and I were playing with chalk on the sidewalk in front of our house, when a neighbor from down the block rode up on her bicycle. We lived in the same subdivision as this woman and we knew who she was, but we had never actually talked with her before. She was an older lady who lived with her elderly parents, and she herself had special needs. She wore her hair in pigtails every day and she rode her beloved bicycle everywhere she went.

She rode up to us and started talking. Tyler and I mostly listened, but we kept drawing. Finally, after about ten minutes of this, I decided we would go inside for a bit to pull ourselves away a bit from the lengthy conversation.

I told Tyler, "Come on, it's time to go in."

He looked at me with puzzlement and confusion. "Aww, Dad," he complained.

"No, son, it's time to go in."

Like the good boy he is, Tyler agreed, but with a sad face, and he began picking up his chalk. I told the lady that we needed to go and would talk to her again another day.

As we packed up and headed inside, she continued to keep talking...and talking...and talking.

Surviving the Trials by Kenny Dietrich

I told Tyler to just tell her good-bye and to have a good day. Eager to please his dad, and like any other good boy, Tyler repeated word for word: "Bye, lady, have a good day."

Still not wavering, she continued to talk. Again, I told Tyler, "Tell her it was nice meeting her." He followed my instructions to the letter and repeated every word I said.

When we finally reached the front door, under my breath I muttered, "She's nuts!" Without missing a beat, Tyler yelled back to the lady, "DAD SAYS YOU'RE NUTS!"

Oh, the mistakes I've made! Trust me when I say I know that calling someone with special needs "nuts" is beyond terrible. For that, I'm truly sorry. She is one of God's creations, and she is beautiful just the way she is. But I wanted to be completely honest with you and not hold anything back about my own mistakes.

I hadn't really learned the lesson yet, but I was about to learn about compassion the hard way.

Being a parent isn't always easy. We must strive to do our best with our children every day. We never know which learning experiences can be crucial in an individual child's development. Children are listening and watching many times when we think they aren't.

I'm not a child psychologist, and I'm not saying I have all the answers about raising children. I'm merely sharing my experience with you. But this doesn't apply to just children...right? It applies to all things in all of our lives.

Colossians 3:23–24 tells us: *"Whatever you do, work heartily, as for the Lord and not for men, knowing that from the Lord you will receive the inheritance as your reward. You are serving the Lord Christ."* This idea is supported earlier in the same chapter of the Bible when the author, Paul, encouraged the church of Colossae to set their minds on things above, not on the things here on the earth. We must all seek first for ourselves the kingdom of Heaven, and then seek to live a life worthy of Jesus' name.

Imagine if we tackled every task in the name of Jesus like we are supposed to. Think about how much better our lives would be, not to mention how it would improve the lives of those around us. Then go a step further than that, and imagine everyone doing this and how it would change the world.

Surviving the Trials by Kenny Dietrich

Every Christian knows they are being watched, and sometimes it feels like we are under a microscope. There is a direct connection between our personal relationship with Jesus and our witness to the rest of the world. You never know who may be watching.

I know this can be extremely difficult during a trial; I know this firsthand. Whether you are going through an illness in your family, or even in your own body, or maybe you are forced to work at a job you don't like, it's difficult to give it your best all the time. God understands this; He knows you are human. Our job here is not to be perfect, but to strive to be more like Christ. Sometimes we fail, but we've still got to keep trying.

5
HOPE

Hebrews 6:19–20 is such a comforting passage of Scripture: *"We have this as a sure and steadfast anchor of the soul, a hope that enters into the inner place behind the curtain, where Jesus has gone as a forerunner on our behalf, having become a high priest forever after the order of Melchizedek."* In this passage, the metaphor of a ship's anchor was used to illustrate security and stability. The curtain referred to represents what used to divide us from communication with God, but Jesus removed that curtain to allow us to talk with God directly. Jesus is the anchor of hope we have in this world and in the afterlife.

Surviving the Trials by Kenny Dietrich

The first time I truly understood the importance of an anchor was when I was in my early twenties and I worked on the river barges as a deckhand. I will never forget my experience with a storm on the river. Although this wasn't the ocean, not even a great sea, it still was more violent and frightening than I had ever imagined. With little to hold on to and even less to stand firmly upon, I was thrashed around by the waves and the wind, which were letting me know who was boss. If it had not been for the barge being anchored, I would have surely been tossed into the raging waters.

With hope in our hearts and minds, we can hold steadfast, knowing that our faith in the Lord will anchor us securely, allowing us to survive any storm. No matter what the obstacle is, we can overcome it.

Surviving the Trials by Kenny Dietrich

Tyler's battle started when he began having trouble seeing the whiteboard at the front of the classroom. His third-grade teacher said he was disrupting the class and having problems focusing. He was moved to the front of the classroom, and he started wearing glasses. Although the glasses helped some with his vision, it did not correct the root of the problem.

Folks, recalling and sharing these stories about the early signs of Tyler's illness is incredibly painful for me to do, as it brings back a flood of emotions and bad memories that I try to keep pushed down inside. It hurts to recount these events, but at the same time, it does get a little easier each time I do so. It also reminds me that, because of my faith in God, I had hope at that time—and I still have that same hope.

Surviving the Trials by Kenny Dietrich

The Bible mentions the word *hope* in 121 different verses, 129 times. With this hope in place, you can survive any trial. Again, Hebrews 10:23 tells us: *"Let us hold fast the confession of our hope without wavering, for he who promised is faithful."*

Looking back, I should have been able to see it coming. During baseball season, the summer before that particular school year, I noticed that Tyler was having trouble catching and hitting the baseball. You've heard the expression, "Keep your eye on the ball"? Well, this described his problem perfectly. He just could not keep his eye on the incoming ball, and this wasn't like him. He had always been a good athlete.

I remember feeling bad for him, because I knew he was trying so hard. It saddens me even more now to think back on it, and I can remember so many of the details.

This particular memory haunts me more than the others. Deep inside, I knew something wasn't right even at that time.

Another recurring incident took place when he would come down from his room upstairs and miss a few steps at the bottom of the steps. One particular time it sounded like he fell down at least four or five steps, and I rushed to see if he was okay. He said that he was, but I responded, "Son! If you don't slow down and straighten up, people are going to think something is wrong with you!" That memory haunts me, too, and it is horrific to think that was my response to him in that situation.

Eventually the problems grew to be more than we could simply dismiss as mere clumsiness or his not paying attention, and so we took him to see his pediatrician, a wonderful man and physician who just also happened to be my pediatrician growing up. After a quick examination, the doctor decided to have a CAT scan done.

We dropped off Madison at my brother's place to play with her cousins, Chelsea and Marisa, while we took Tyler to the hospital for his test. We didn't know what was ahead of us at this time, but we knew that a trial was for all of us, and it has made all of our relationships stronger as a result. To this day, the bond the cousins share is unbreakable.

We were told that the testing was being done "just to rule out the worst-case scenario." I no longer like that saying at all, and I try not to use it myself. And what started out as a routine scan ended up becoming a full CAT scan performed with intravenous dye, which made us concerned.

And then worry and panic started to creep in.

When the nurse came to us and to say that they needed to do more scans with the dye, I asked what was wrong.

The nurse said she wasn't allowed to tell us anything, that the doctors were the only ones allowed to do so. But I could see what was going on in her facial expression...in her eyes as the tears started to pool. Our world was turning upside down.

After hours of agonizing in the waiting room, we were finally released and sent on our way like nothing had happened. Now it was a waiting game. Although it seemed like forever, we actually didn't have to wait very long. Our pediatrician himself called and asked to see us in his office right away. By this time, it was late in the day, going on nine o'clock at night. I knew this couldn't be good news.

After dropping Tyler off at my brother's place to hang out with the rest of the kids, we met the doctor at his office. He turned on a few lights, then he led us to a break room, where we sat at a table and he gave us the bad news. "Tyler has a brain tumor."

I cannot express in words the horrible feeling of hearing that your child has been diagnosed with cancer. It is a parent's worst nightmare, accompanied by a storm of uncertainty.

Tyler's pediatrician had a resource book of recommended hospitals and surgeons. He opened it on the table and pointed to the name of one the best neurological surgeons in the United States. This surgeon was only a couple hours' drive away. It was decided that we should take immediate action by calling the next morning to try and get Tyler in to see this man. Our pediatrician would call to make the appointment as soon as possible, and we would make preparations to take leave of our work, to travel, and to get Tyler the best possible medical care.

With a game plan now formulated, we left the office and I drove straight to my boss's house to inform him of the news. At the time, I was selling insurance in downtown Ashland, and I'll always be grateful to the man for whom I worked for his understanding during this period in my life. I cried on his shoulder as I explained the situation. Once again God had put me in the right place, with the right people, at the right time.

Surviving the Trials by Kenny Dietrich

After we picked up the kids, both of whom were now at my brother's house, we made it back to our home to break the news to Tyler himself. His mother and I sat him down on the couch to explain things to him the best we could. I explained to Tyler what was going on in his body, that the cause of the headaches and the problems with his eyes was a brain tumor. I went on to tell him that the doctors would have to take the tumor out the best way they knew how.

"Will it hurt?" he asked with widened eyes. I told him no, that it wouldn't, and that he would be asleep while they did it. Tears formed in the corners of his blue eyes, and his chin began to quiver. "Will I have to get a shot?"

Now tears formed in my eyes, as I answered that yes, he would, but I reassured him that his mother and I would be there with him the entire time. Then I apologized for not being able to fix this, and told him I was sorry if I had been hard on him lately; I hadn't realized it wasn't his fault, that the illness had been the cause of all of his behavior problems.

I will never forget his response: "Don't be sorry, Dad...you're the best dad ever." I then cried like a baby. At eight years old, Tyler was wise beyond his years.

Tyler slept in bed with us that night, but I don't think anyone of us actually slept. We talked most of the night and prayed when we weren't talking. Early the next morning, Tyler's mother was on the phone trying to get in to see the neurosurgeon. With patience and persistence, she got an appointment to see him the same day, later in the afternoon.

Surviving the Trials by Kenny Dietrich

We needed to request a copy of Tyler's slides from the CAT scans performed at the children's hospital. Without these there would be no way the surgeon could give an assessment. The problem was, we didn't have them, and we had no idea if we could get them in time. If not, however, we would have to postpone the appointment and thus delay his treatment.

Thanks be to God, a friend of ours worked closely enough with this part of the hospital that she was able to get the copies we needed right away. We literally picked them up from her on the road next to the hospital as she stood on the sidewalk and handed them to us through the car window. This was done after we had packed quickly, loaded up the kids, and were on our way to the children's hospital two hours away. I'm sure rules were broken and bent to make that happen, but thankfully nothing was ever said about it. If you've ever dealt with getting medical records from a hospital, you might ask how we accomplished this in such a short time. I never asked why or how it worked; I simply recognized it was God's hand at work.

I wasn't where I should have been with God at this time in my life, but this trial had renewed my faith. I began to pray again like I hadn't in years, and I found hope in God's promises. The Bible is full of hope. Romans 15:13 tells us: *"May the God of hope fill you with all joy and peace in believing, so that by the power of the Holy Spirit you may abound in hope."*

Tyler was admitted to the hospital, and the night before his surgery, he met the doctor who would be taking care of him after the initial operation. This doctor was

Surviving the Trials by Kenny Dietrich

in his final year of residency, a young man whom we affectionately called Dr. Mike. He gave Tyler a routine exam while we all watched. He listened to his chest, felt his stomach, and looked at his arms, legs, and feet. Tyler watched with great interest, even asking, "Why are you looking at my feet? They tell me the problem is in my head." Dr. Mike laughed uncontrollably, and this was the beginning of a beautiful friendship.

Children's hospitals are places of both sadness and happiness. They are sad because so many sick children are among us and yet we spend so much time, energy, and money on meaningless activities instead of helping one another. But they are happy places, too, full of hope, providing great care. Many kids even get well again, and for those children who don't make it, the children's hospitals provide tremendous comfort.

How does that hit you, knowing that some children will go in the hospital but won't make it out? It hurt me then, and it still does today—beyond words. If you've never been to a children's hospital, I highly recommend that you visit or volunteer. Or maybe you could help out at a Ronald McDonald House; they also do great things and that's a good place to start.

The next day was Tyler's surgery. To be honest, I can't remember what time of day it was when we all gathered in the waiting room. There were family and friends and lots of prayers. We accompanied Tyler back into the surgery suite as far as we could go, all the way to the operating room swing doors, where another of the moments in my life took place that I will never forget. Having to let go of my son, not knowing what the outcome would be, has been one of the hardest things I've ever had to do. If it were not for my faith in Jesus and the hope He gives to us all, I could have never handed Tyler over to the surgeons in that room.

6
THE LORD'S WILL

After eight hours of surgery someone from the medical team finally came out to tell us that Tyler had made it through the surgery successfully. The doctor wanted to see my wife and me to give us a recap of the surgery. In the consult room, the surgeon gave us the news that the surgery had been successful although it had gone longer than expected. They were able to remove more of the tumor than they'd originally expected. The surgeon went on to explain that almost all of the tumor had been removed from Tyler's brain. God is so good!

Tyler was moved to the ICU, where he would spend some time recovering, but we were allowed to spend time with him there.

When we got to his bedside, he was sleeping like an angel. The nurse told us he had been awake previously, but he was in and out. I laid my hand gently on his back and whispered his name softly: "Tyler."

Without moving or even opening his eyes, Tyler gave a long, sweet, drawn-out "Yeah…"

"Hey, buddy, it's Dad. Mom and I are here with you." He replied with a simple "okay" and then went back to sleep. This would be the very last time we heard "this" voice. After that night, what the medical community calls "cranial mutism" set in, and Tyler would have to learn to talk all over again.

Several days later, I received a call from Tyler's pediatrician's office. The office worker stated that he had secured Tyler an appointment with the neurosurgeon for the next week. I laughed and told them that Tyler had already had the surgery and was recovering in the ICU. The phone went silent for several beats, and then the man asked with disbelief in his voice, "How did you do that?"

Apparently, he had done all he could to get the soonest surgeon appointment available, and a week away was the best he could do on his own. I understood perfectly that God had blazed the trail before us.

After a few weeks in the ICU, Tyler was moved to a regular room and returned to the care of Dr. Mike. Here he would undergo multiple types of therapy and treatments—including animal therapy, which, by the way, I thought was amazing. In animal therapy, the therapist brings in a well-trained animal, usually a dog, and lets the patient spend some time petting it, giving and receiving love. You'd be surprised how much this brightens their day. After that I was, and still am, open to any type of therapy that proves beneficial.

Once he was back in a regular room, Tyler had to relearn most of his everyday activities, such as talking, walking, and using the bathroom, all of the little things most of us take for granted. I recall the first time after surgery when he smiled and laughed. He had "tooted" *very* loudly and he began to laugh. We all laughed with him, until we began to cry from the happiness. After all, it's the little things in life that matter the most.

Undergoing brain surgery is a lot like having a stroke. Tyler couldn't speak, he didn't have full use or movement of his hands and arms, and he couldn't walk. It was a long road stretching ahead of him.

Some mornings I got the opportunity to get up and go to see Tyler before everyone else. I got up early and made my trek from the Ronald McDonald House to the hospital across the street. I will never forget one particular morning, not just because it had snowed an additional four inches on top of what had already accumulated, but because of the events that unfolded.

I liked getting to Tyler's room in time to help him with his breakfast. While feeding him his scrambled eggs that day, I started to notice a change in Tyler. He went from all smiles and happily eating his food, to barely chewing, and he started staring off over my shoulder in the distance. I tried calling to him, but he suddenly wouldn't respond. I called for the nurse, and moments later she rushed in and asked, "How long has he been like this?" I explained that the changes had just happened while I had been feeding him.

She checked his vitals and started inspecting all of his lines and ports. She then called for the doctor. Two more people rushed into the room, another nurse and Dr. Mike. They all worked quickly to determine what was going on, but honestly, they weren't sure what was happening.

Once again, they asked me to tell them exactly what had just transpired. I repeated the events the best I could, exactly the way I remembered. They then went back to the drain line coming from his head and started drawing fluids.

As the doctors and nurses rushed around, I called Tyler's mother and grandmother who were still at the Ronald

McDonald House. I asked them to come over to the hospital as quickly as possible. By the time they arrived, Tyler had declined dramatically. Eventually they would quarantine Tyler's room and keep everyone in it who had entered, until a contagious disease could be ruled out. This quarantine went on for the better part of an hour.

During this time, while we were closed off from the rest of the hospital, we could do nothing but sit and wait. We knew that Tyler's condition was growing worse and worse, and that there was no cause or cure in sight. One of our favorite nurses was quarantined with us, and therefore she wasn't allowed to leave his room either.

The room was still and quiet; only the sounds of Tyler's monitors could be heard. We all had been praying during this time, but now our prayers started to become audible. I don't know who the first person was to start praying out loud, but before it was all over, we had each taken a turn begging God to save this little boy.

Tyler's fever had risen to 104 degrees, his heart rate become dangerously slow, and his blood pressure was dropping. He was close to death, and we all knew it. Even our strong and courageous nurse began to cry for this little guy.

I tried once again: "Heavenly Father, we come to You begging for healing. Please heal Tyler. Lord, we want him to stay with us. Please don't take him away."

A doctor with whom I wasn't familiar came in dressed head to toe in protective clothing and a mask. We all looked at him in anticipation. Without a word, he looked at the monitors, checked Tyler's lines and ports, and then left the room. Nothing.

The room stayed quiet. It felt like the doctor had just taken all of the hope out of the room when he left. *Lord, why won't You help him?* I thought to myself. As I looked around the room, I could tell the others were starting to feel the same way. It had been almost two long, terrible hours, and I was mentally, emotionally, and spiritually exhausted.

Then it hit me like a revelation: God wanted us to trust in Him! He wanted us to know that He has our best interest in His mind and heart. So, I did. I prayed out loud, "Heavenly Father, maybe I'm going about this the wrong way. Instead of praying so desperately for healing, I should be praying for Your will—for Your will to be done. We hand Tyler over to You, Lord.

Take him to be with You or heal him to live on earth with us. Either way, we know that You have what is best for all of us in mind, including Tyler. Thank You, Lord, for Your goodness and mercy. Amen."

The room stayed quiet for several moments, except for a few sniffles and the beep of the monitor. But peace and calm had replaced the anxiety and worry. I can't speak for the rest of the people who were there, but I could feel the Holy Spirit in the room with us, and it felt like a warm hug.

Only a few minutes later, the door flew open and Dr. Mike appeared, rejoicing. "We found it! We know what is causing this," he exclaimed. Immediately he and another doctor started hanging up bags of antibiotics. They moved around the room with urgency and precision. In less than an hour, Tyler was back to smiling and responding to us.

The book of Matthew tells us of Jesus' prayer in Gethsemane: "*My Father, if it be possible, let this cup pass from me*" (26:39). But before that, Jesus had asked His Father whether or not it was possible to do it another way. Matthew 26:39 gives the details: "*And going a little farther he fell on his face and prayed, saying, My Father, if it be possible, let this cup pass from me.*" Why is this information so important? Because it shows us that it is okay to be human. Jesus went on to say, "*Nevertheless, not as I will, but as you will*" (verse 39).

For me, this passage is special. It shows me that even Jesus admits that the spirit is strong and willing, but our flesh is weak. He was being honest, and this was an agonizing time for Him. But there are

Surviving the Trials by Kenny Dietrich

some important things to understand in this story of Jesus praying there in the olive groves.

First, He didn't want to be alone. That is why He asked Peter, James, and John to walk with Him that evening. In the same way, neither should we try to make it through the trials alone. It is okay to ask for help from the church, support groups, counselors, close friends, or whomever else you choose to have your back. It's okay to participate in a support group or to see counselor (as long as they are Christ-centered). A big part of our survival lies in the community.

Second, Jesus prayed more than once to ask God for another way out. Once again, this shows that it's okay to be human. It's okay to have feelings of dread or uncertainty. We shouldn't let them take over our lives or control our faith, but they are, for the most part, normal. Through the years I've gone through some counseling, and I found it very helpful—not because I was "crazy"; rather, on the contrary, to be reminded that *I wasn't*.

Finally, Jesus established God's will as more important than our own. So often our fleshly desires and our human wants take over, and we forget to ask for the Lord's will to be done. He knows what's best for us, and if we let Him, He will take care of us and show us the way. Proverbs 3:5–6 states: *"Trust in the L*ORD *with all your heart, and do not lean on your own understanding. In all your ways acknowledge him, and he will make straight your paths."*

I've learned so much from the trials in my life. This one taught me about the

Lord's will and how God knows the bigger picture. This trial was, quite possibly, the worst thing I'd ever had to endure. I don't believe God "tests" us, or purposely gives us these trials—they just happen—but He is always there to help us through. This is just part of life and the journey, and everyone's perception of the journey is different.

Occasionally I have had to remind myself that not everyone sees things the way I do. One of my most memorable examples of how people perceive things differently from me is the first time I went backpacking. I took my brother, Chris, picked a forest close to us, and mapped out a sixteen-mile-long trail. First, this far too many miles for a couple of novices. I was used to wilderness camping with my Air National Guard squadron, but backpacking and bivouacking are two different things. With backpacking you have no support, and whatever you're going to need for the trip you have to carry literally on your back.

We hiked the better part of the day, and by late afternoon we had reached the thirteen-mile marker. Deciding to enjoy the evening, we set up camp early and relaxed. Little did I realize that we had actually started the trail at the end and we were working our way backward. Yep, so the next day we ended up doing thirteen miles back to the car. It was brutal.

After that, though, I was hooked! However, from Chris's perspective, it was miserable. He decided never to do it again. I don't think (or at least I hope) I didn't ruin it for him. I think I might have just reinforced what he already thought it would be like.

My perspective, however, was completely different: I wanted to do it again, and do it better. I loved the wilderness, the sights, the sounds, even the discomfort from the punishing exercise. Looking back on the trials in my life, I also have a different view of the struggles I went through than I did when they were happening.

7
MORE TRIALS AHEAD

James 1:2–3 states: *"Count it all joy, my brothers, when you meet trials of various kinds, for you know that the testing of your faith produces steadfastness."* I'm not new to trials. I know firsthand how badly they can hurt, some more than others. I know how hard it is to "count it all joy" during them, but the point James is trying to make here is that these trials can make us better if we allow them to.

Starting with the initial surgery and the time Tyler spent in the ICU, and then in a normal hospital room, then his return for another brain surgery, Tyler would ultimately spend a total of seventy-seven days in the children's hospital. The second surgery he underwent was to install a ventriculoperitoneal (VP) shunt. This is a medical device that relieves pressure on the brain caused by the accumulation of excess cerebrospinal fluid in the brain's ventricles, thus preventing hydrocephalus. From there, Tyler would undergo weeks of radiation therapy, focusing on his head and spine, another brutal regimen of treatments.

The radiation was delivered to his spine while he was lying facedown on his stomach. The force of the radiation was so powerful that it passed all the way through his body, blistering him on the outside (as well as on the inside) of his chest.

During this treatment, I was already back to work and traveling back and forth to the hospital on the weekends. I felt bad about not being able to be there every day, but the people taking care of Tyler, a husband and wife team, both nurses, were wonderful to him during his treatment. They were good people whom God had placed in our path to help us through another trying time.

Tyler was eventually released and sent home after these seventy-seven days; he would continue his physical therapy and begin chemotherapy at a hospital close to home. One part of our journey was behind us, and we were ready to move forward to finish the rest of his treatments. The outlook for Tyler's future was now positive. Once again, God had shown us His goodness, mercy, and grace. This part of my life was the hardest I'd ever been through, but it increased my strength for future trials to come.

In Romans 8:18, the apostle Paul wrote these words: *"For I consider that the suffer-*

ings of this present time are not worth comparing with the glory that is to be revealed to us."

Even though we may do our best to live the way the Bible tells us to, we are still going to experience trials. Know three things about what you are going through. First, this isn't the first trial you've been through and it won't be the last. Second, how you respond to your trial is what makes you who you are; this is the fire that will temper you. And finally, God goes before you. Deuteronomy 31:8 states: *"It is the L*ORD *who goes before you. He will be with you; he will not leave you or forsake you. Do not fear or be dismayed."*

I think that 100 years from now, the world of medicine will look back on chemotherapy as the most barbaric form of medicine ever practiced. That is, if we can get past all of the money it makes, and therein lies the real problem. Tyler was to receive the chemotherapy protocol for his specific type of cancer at a hospital a thirty-minute drive away. This hospital would work closely with the children's hospital where he had had his initial surgery.

In this part of the journey, we met more wonderful people whom God placed in our path, including nurses, doctors, and even other patients.

Tyler became friends with the kids he met, and they would play and talk during their treatments. He became the closest to a boy named Daniel. They hit it off from the moment they met, and they shared the same type of cancer. Daniel's dad said that Daniel actually looked forward to his treatments so that he could play with Tyler. Imagine looking forward to chemotherapy! Kids don't know they are "sick" with cancer; they look at it as more of an inconvenience. It is merely another obstacle to growing up.

It's all in the attitude. I have a close friend who has been battling cancer for years. His faith is amazing, and his attitude is like none I have ever seen. I don't look at him as "sick" with cancer; instead, I see a man with obstacles he constantly overcomes. My friend is winning his fight, and he cannot lose. He wins no matter what, either here on earth or in heaven.

This was a difficult time for us all. Chemotherapy is hard on everyone. It eats away at everything, especially the patient. I began to lose track of time and what day it was. We lost income from missing days at work, leaving early for appointments, and the expense of traveling. You can easily lose focus of who you are and what you're doing in a situation like this. Cancer not only affects the patient; it affects everyone around them, too.

When the chemo was over, we threw a party as most cancer survivors do. God had pulled us through another crisis. I won't write about the entire chemotherapy experience, because most people have a good idea what goes on. However, you cannot understand the full magnitude of it unless you have gone through it firsthand. It is my prayer that you will never have to.

Through God's blessings, Tyler began to recover. He was starting to walk again, he speech was improving, and even his motor skills were returning. It was a happy time for all of us. People have made full recoveries from these kinds of tumors and go on to lead long, productive, and happy lives.

Surviving the Trials by Kenny Dietrich

Through all the fear, anger, and helplessness, God still prevailed.

Why does God allow bad things to happen to good people? This is one of the most difficult questions to answer in the Christian faith. However, once God has shown you this answer, you might never ask the question again. I know that once this answer was revealed to me, I stopped asking "why" and started noticing the situation as simply a trial of life.

Most of the time, once you are past the trial you can look back on it and begin to understand where God was leading you. A trial is just a trail, leading you to a better spiritual life. John 15:1–2 tells us: *"I am the true vine, and my Father is the vinedresser. Every branch in me that does not bear fruit he takes away, and every branch that does bear fruit he prunes, that it may* bear more fruit." Again, Jesus said in John 16:33, *"I have said these things to you, that in me you may have peace. In the world you will have tribulation. But take heart; I have overcome the world."* In Jesus's farewell discourse to the disciples, He reassured them of the victory.

About a year after the chemo treatments had ended, during a periodic checkup Tyler's scans showed some unusual activity. This called for more scans and more tests. The doctors eventually determined that he had experienced a recurrence of the cancer. The images of his brain and spine showed many small spots of illumination that were indicative of cancer. In Tyler's particular type of cancer, a recurrence is very deadly, with only a five percent chance of survival. We were convinced by the doctor that our only alternative was to enlist in a clinical trial involving a new type of chemotherapy that wasn't on the market yet but was still just in its testing phase. We signed Tyler's life away after we read through all the paperwork, especially the list of potential side effects. It was the only option we had left.

Tyler went through nine weeks of this chemotherapy, but it had no effect on the cancer in his body according to the scans and reports. His health continued to deteriorate, and yet he also began to show all the side effects that had been predicted for this clinical trial. He was losing his hearing, he lost all of the motor control that he had gained back, and his brain activity was impaired. The doctors finally told to consider "compassionate care" in order to ease his passing. After all we had been through, the medical community was ready to give up on him. To be honest, I, too, had reached the end of my strength.

Although I wasn't ready to see Tyler go, a part of me was starting to accept that it was inevitable.

If it hadn't been for the faith and determination of Tyler's mother, he would have died. But she refused to give up and somehow found the strength and the foresight to do some research of her own. With her own limited resources, Heather started digging the research on this particular type of cancer and its treatments. She then started contacting any hospitals and doctors whom she she thought might help in any way she could. Through e-mails, phone calls, and snail mail, she put Tyler's information out there. She sent copies of Tyler's medical records and reports to anyone who would take a look at them, to anyone who would listen to our distress call. It was our last SOS.

Surviving the Trials by Kenny Dietrich

St. Jude Children's Research Hospital reached out to us as if they were someone on a boat throwing out a life-preserver to a drowning man. "We would love to meet with you," they said. "We don't even think he has cancer." I'm paraphrasing, of course, but this was the gist of it. They had looked at his scans, and they recognized the illuminated spots as white matter regrowth in the nervous system. In layman's terms, Tyler's brain was actually trying to heal itself. This diagnosis was still a cutting-edge one in the field, and very few others recognized it as valid.

As a matter of record, the hospital from which Tyler had received his chemotherapy dismissed this new diagnosis as "unfounded." They told us that Tyler would not be treated well at St. Jude's, that he would only be considered as a research subject, or just another number. I am not making this up. The hospital even delayed releasing Tyler's medical records and fought our transfer the whole way. Little did I know, they actually had something to hide.

Surviving the Trials by Kenny Dietrich

8
GOD'S PEOPLE STEP UP

The apostle Paul got word that the church in Galatia was having problems after he left, but he did not regard this as defeat. In Paul's letter to the Galatians, he wrote, "*Bear one another's burdens, and so fulfill the law of Christ*" (Galatians 6:2). To "bear one another's burdens" is to become more Christlike and emulate Jesus, the ultimate Burden-Bearer. After all, isn't that our main goal, to be more Christlike?

If you've never been to St. Jude Children's Research Hospital, I highly recommend a visit or a tour. It is heartbreaking to see how these kids suffer the way they do, but it is also uplifting to see that great people are willing to help bear these kinds of burdens. If there has to be such a terrible thing as pediatric cancer, at least there is a wonderful place that carries the mission of providing the latest medicine and research, while freeing families from the burden of the cost of such lifesaving health care. You'll probably arrive and cry for the first hour that you are there, but when you leave you'll have a big smile plastered across your face.

We parked in the underground parking garage at the hospital and found our way to the reception area. The kind man behind the desk checked us in, and after getting us taken care of, he handed me a check. Before I even opened it to look at it, I asked him what I was supposed to do with it, whether it was to be sent to my insurance company.

"No," he replied with a smile. "That is yours to keep, you know, for your travel expenses."

I was shocked and amazed. Of all the places I'd been over the last year with Tyler, always handing over my cash or waiting for the bill to later come in the mail, this was the first time anyone had given me any money for our expenses. I guess I stood there a bit in disbelief, because he had to speak to free me from my trance. "It's because of your mileage," he said as he glanced at his computer screen. "Yeah, you came all the way from Ashland, Kentucky, right?"

"Yes...yes, we did. I'm just not used to hospitals handing me a check. It's usually the other way around."

He rested his elbows on the desk, folded his hands, and gave another warm smile.

"We get that a lot. We'll take your insurance information and bill them for what we can, but you'll never get the first bill from us. Whatever your insurance doesn't pay, we absorb."

I vowed that once I reached a point in my life where I could again afford to donate any of my personal money to a charity, I would gladly give to this incredible place.

Tyler spent the next three months in and out of St. Jude Children's Hospital getting the treatments he needed, including hyperbaric oxygen treatments. This therapy uses a chamber, set up like an indoor submarine, to deliver 100 percent oxygen to the body at an ambient pressure higher than the atmospheric pressure, removing any bubbles and excess dissolved gas. If you research this particular treatment, you will see the numerous conditions it can improve and sometimes cure. Tyler literally went from about to enter "compassionate care" to getting ready to go back to school.

Everyone can benefit from this type of treatment at some point in their lives, but the powers that be have decided it would be too expensive for social insurance plans such as Medicare, and of course, private insurance companies followed suit. That's just my opinion, but I have seen the amazing results in my son's body with my own eyes. If St. Jude Children's Hospital and the good people there hadn't got Tyler in for this treatment, my insurance probably wouldn't have approved it and Tyler would not have lived.

First John 3:16–17 tells us, *"By this we know love, that he laid down his life for us, and we ought to lay down our lives for the brothers. But if anyone has the world's goods and sees his brother in need, yet closes his heart against him, how does God's love abide in him?"* The "love" to which John is referring is Jesus's sacrifice on the cross, His act of selflessness and a way of life in which self-giving is paramount. The "world's goods" here refers to our treasure that is not stored in heaven. The things we think we own in this world are only temporary. Understand that we are only stewards of the things we have been given on the earth. Even money itself is just a tool to be used for God's missions and tasks and for advancing His kingdom and inviting people to heaven.

During one Sunday morning church service, I felt compelled to give my tithe. Times were tough at that point, and Tyler's care was taking its financial toll on our family. All I had was a twenty-dollar bill in my wallet, and it needed to last us until the following Friday. Our bills were paid up, but there was no extra money to be found anywhere. As I pulled the money out to place it in the offering plate, I literally felt sick to my stomach. I started to pull it back toward my wallet, but then that still, small voice inside of me told me that everything would be alright.

So, I placed the money in the plate and watched as it was passed on down the aisle. Even though I'd given my last dollar bitterly, I still felt at peace and I knew that somehow, someway, God would work everything out. I enjoyed the rest of the church service and was thankful I was there. After we were dismissed, while on my way out of the church, a woman stopped me on the steps. "I wanted you to know that we are praying for you and that we love you all," she said as she grabbed my hand and shook it. As she walked away, I realized that she had slipped a note into the palm of my hand. I turned my hand over and opened my fingers to see a one-hundred-dollar bill resting in my hand. You can't outgive God!

Once again, God had placed people in my life to help me, and because I was on the road He wanted me to travel, His people stepped up to meet our needs.

Philippians 2:4 reassures us: *"Let each of you look not only to his own interest, but also to the interests of others."* Always be looking for opportunities to help others. It is clearly written in the Bible that we are called to help each other. This doesn't always have to involve huge assistance; help comes in many forms. It may require giving until it hurts, or it may involve something as simple as sending a message to someone saying, "I'm thinking of and praying for you."

Surviving the Trials by Kenny Dietrich

9
FRIENDSHIP

Early one morning, about five o'clock to be more precise, I received a phone call from the father of one of the children who had had chemotherapy with Tyler. When I answered the call, I did not immediately recognize the number, until the voice on the other end said, "Mr. Dietrich, this is Daniel's daddy. He wanted me to call you." Groggily and without thinking first, I asked how he was doing. Daniel's dad then said, "He passed away."

Now I was wide-awake, lying in bed looking up at the ceiling, feeling terrible for this father and Daniel's family. A hundred thoughts rushed through my mind. I wondered when it had happened: maybe last week, maybe a month ago? So I asked. "I'm so sorry. When did he pass?"

Daniel's father said, "About twenty minutes ago."

I sat straight up in bed, my heart pounding with the realization of what had just happened. One of the last things on this dying child's mind was his friend—my son, Tyler. How was this even possible? They were just children. And that was when I understood the power of friendship.

Ecclesiastes 4:9–10 tells us, *"Two are better than one, because they have a good reward for their toil. For if they fall, one will lift up his fellow. But woe to him who is alone when he falls and has not another to lift him up!"* A person who is smart will choose to work with someone else, or even a team of others, to accomplish his goal rather than trying to do it by himself.

Sometimes each of us needs that kind of support, and there is no one better to provide it than a dear friend. The same goes for providing that support for someone else in your life.

Some of the greatest Christian fellowship and counseling I have ever had in my life came from evening walks taken with a fellow brother in Christ. I hope and pray that I was some help and comfort to my Christian brother, because he was so much help and comfort to me. These walks gave me inspiration, courage, and occasionally even tough love.

Sometimes we don't know what to say, but just being there is usually enough. Job had three friends who tried to come to his aid during his time of trial. They came together to show him sympathy and offer comfort. Job was doing so badly that when they saw him from a distance, they didn't even recognize him: *"And they raised their voices and wept, and they tore their robes and sprinkled dust on their heads toward heaven. And they sat with him on the ground seven days and seven nights, and no one spoke a word to him, for they saw that his suffering was very great"* (Job 2:12–13). During our trials, it is so important to surround ourselves with good, godly people.

Friendship is a theme echoed again in Proverbs 27:17, one of my favorite verses: *"Iron sharpens iron, and one man sharpens another."* If you were to take a file and try to sharpen an ax, the metal in the file will be harder than the metal in the ax, and therefore it will grind it down to a fine edge. Even though the file is stronger, it cannot cut wood. But without the file to sharpen the ax, it can't cut wood very well, either. Instead, by using both properly, you can split wood with efficiency all day long. So not only is important to have friends, but it is also important to have friends who aren't afraid to hold you accountable to God's standards.

Surviving the Trials by Kenny Dietrich

10
YOU ARE NOT ALONE

Hebrews 13:8 tells us, *"Jesus Christ is the same yesterday and today and forever."* Like the old song says, "What a friend we have in Jesus!" He will always be there for you; He will never leave you. We will leave Him long before He would ever leave us. Although it might not feel like it sometimes, He is always there.

We later ended up moving to the beautiful town of Hernando, Mississippi, about a half hour's drive from Memphis, Tennessee, and St. Jude Children's Hospital. My wife's uncle worked for the railroad, and he told us that they were always hiring good workers. So, I applied, was tested, and got a new job as a railroad conductor.

Surviving the Trials by Kenny Dietrich

Things were going well for us there in Mississippi. I had a really good job, a beautiful home, and Tyler was on the mend. He and Madison were also in a good school and doing well.

And that's when it happened. Heather and I had allowed the trial we had been through to take its toll and lead us down the wrong path. We lost sight of what was important, and worst of all, I lost the faith to which I'd held so strongly during those dark times. In my experience, the serious illness or loss of a child can either make a couple's bond unbreakable or it can drive a wedge between them.

Because of this we had been growing apart and allowed the last few years of heartache to come between us. Ultimately, we split up. We had an amicable divorce and she left taking the kids with her the way we agreed upon.

I was now working a job I didn't care for, even though I was making good money and still living in a beautiful house I was miserable. This was another of life's lessons that I learned the hard way. Money is only a tool. It allows us to buy the things that we need, and it can even better our lives if we make good decisions with it. But it cannot solve everything. Eventually the loneliness took over, and I looked for and found a new girlfriend.

I was heading down the wrong path and I knew it. I hurt so badly during this time, and I was miserable. The further away from God and family I moved, the worse things seemed to become. Finally, I hit rock bottom, where I had never felt so alone.

Surviving the Trials by Kenny Dietrich

The good thing about hitting rock bottom, though, is that there is nowhere to go but up. I remember being at my wits' end, while looking at myself in the bathroom mirror. I didn't even look like myself anymore. Who was this stranger? The anger, the emotional trauma, and all of my horrible feelings had taken over my appearance. I didn't like the person I saw in the mirror anymore, and I even contemplated suicide at that point. It was then that I knew I needed to do something right away; I could wait no longer. I packed up the old car that I had been left with what I needed to survive, and I headed home, back to Ashland, Kentucky.

I called my employer in Memphis and requested some vacation time. This would take the first full week of vacation I had earned—and I was taking it in January. But I knew I couldn't live the way I'd been living anymore. I needed to get back home. During that week of vacation, my goal was to search for employment back in Kentucky.

Once again God had placed good—no, *great*—people in my life to show me that I wasn't alone. Even though I wasn't following His direction at that time, He was still lighting my way. I called a few friends back in my hometown, looking for any kind of work I could find. A good friend of mine Brad said he would have something for me in a few days. When I told him what was going on, the first thing he said without hesitation was, "What do you need? Money? A place to stay? You name it, brother, and I will help you." Now, that is a true friend. He came through for me quickly and then connected me with another saint, Mrs. Linda.

I will always be grateful and indebted to both of these wonderful people. Mrs. Linda has such a charitable heart and she loves helping other people. She is a fine Christian woman who will always hold a special place in my heart.

But put me to work, she did. I worked "extreme" labor for her, shoveling, carrying, and processing coal. I can honestly say that I have shoveled coal for a living! It was hard work, but it was honest work. At the end of the day it was what I needed at that time in my life.

Mrs. Linda treated me like a son and she rewarded me for my hard work and efforts. I earned her trust and soon became supervisor of my department. Not only did Mrs. Linda save me financially, she helped to save me spiritually. She was a great example of how a Christian should conduct themselves in the business world.

My trials were far from over, but things were starting to look up for me again. Jeremiah 29:11 has always reminded me of God's goodness: *"For I know the plans I have for you, declares the LORD, plans for welfare and not for evil, to give you a future and a hope."* There is so much to learn from this passage, but first let's take a look at "the plans" God has for us. That means *you*! Yes, that's right, the almighty God of the universe knows who you are, and He has an individual plan for each of us. To me that is simply amazing. Next, look at His "plans for welfare"—not for "evil." God may allow things to happen to us that we don't understand, but it's never for evil. It is always for what is ultimately best for our well-being. Lastly, the words "a future and a hope" refers to having peace in your home and heart. Here, God is looking to your future, even though so many times I think we forget that He can see what lies ahead. When there are times of peace in our homes and hearts, we are to recognize them and cherish them.

I had started to rebuild my life, one piece at a time. However, I did end up filing bankruptcy because the pile of debt and Tyler's medical bills were simply too much for me to ever recover from. This is not something I'm ashamed of, because help like the concept of bankruptcy had been designed for just such a purpose. The people who abuse the system should be ashamed of themselves for giving the honest people who need the system a bad name.

I lived in a one-room apartment for a little over a year as I rebuilt my credit score.

Surviving the Trials by Kenny Dietrich

I continued to work for Mrs. Linda and I also worked a couple of side jobs cutting grass and putting up drywall to make ends meet. Eventually I started to get my head above water and was enjoying life again. It had been so long since I had been happy that I had almost forgotten what it was like.

During this time, I saw the kids whenever I could, but they were constantly on the move with their mother and their new stepfather, with him being in the army. I realized during this period in my life how important it was to take care of myself. One of my favorite analogies can be seen when the airline attendant explains, "Before you can help others, you must first put the oxygen mask on yourself."

My mother, now a widow for the second time, offered to help me buy a house—a fixer-upper, for thirty-five thousand dollars. When we took a tour of it, the Realtor literally held her nose because the smell was so bad. There was no electricity upstairs, and there was no air-conditioning at all. The house was soon to be condemned if it didn't sell. But what I saw was a diamond in the rough. It had been built in the 1930s, it was made solid, and the location was perfect. This project would keep me busy for the next couple of years while God continued to bless me and my hard work.

As you might be able to tell, I wasn't looking to get back into another romantic relationship. I was focused on my jobs, repairing my credit, and renovating my old house. But God had other plans for me. I agreed to a blind date set up by one of my good friends. She and her husband had become great friends to me during this time of my life. I spent many evenings with them eating their food and hanging out with them watching TV shows and movies.

I had been on plenty of dates since my divorce, but no one had really made me want to settle down again. I had determined to be a bachelor for the rest of my life, and at that point I was enjoying it. That is, until "she" came along, on the third date. Yes, you read that right, it wasn't until the third date that I realized that this girl was different—and special.

Elisha was not like any other women I'd ever gone out with. She was a beautiful, strong single mother to a smart and cute three-year-old named Layla. Elisha shared my offbeat sense of humor, which was a "must" for someone to be able to put up with me. Over the course of the next few months, she became my best friend and confidant. We tied the knot after about a year of dating, during a simple but wonderful service at the church in which I had grown up. I was surrounded by my family and my closest friends, and the service was officiated by the pastor who had counseled me after I returned home a few years before.

This was a turning point for both of us, not just in life itself, but in our spiritual lives. We had found a church together, one we both loved and agreed on. We still attend regularly and pray together daily. We began our new life together with God in the center. I felt great, and I knew that with Elisha as my companion, together we could overcome anything.

John 16:33 states: *"I have said these things to you, that in me you may have peace. In the world you will have tribula-*

tion. But take heart; I have overcome the world." God created us in His own image, to walk with Him and talk with Him each day. God has shown me that He is always there, and He will put people in your life along the journey to reassure you of this fact.

Surviving the Trials by Kenny Dietrich

11
HEALING

Philippians 2:12–13 speaks to my heart: *"Therefore, my beloved, as you have always obeyed, so now, not only as in my presence but much more in my absence, work out your own salvation with fear and trembling, for it is God who works in you, both to will and to work for his good pleasure."* The "fear and trembling" mentioned here refers to "living good," or "living right," according to the Christian tenets of faith. The desire to live good, or live right, comes from God. The apostle Paul was stating that with His help, we can be good enough to merit God's favor. Because of God's love and grace, He will work out the good behavior, or right living, through us.

Surviving the Trials by Kenny Dietrich

I wanted to give back, to return to all those who gave to me during my times of trial. So, with the encouragement of my wife and with the help of my good friend and boss, Mrs. Linda, I founded a 501(c)3 nonprofit charity to help children with pediatric cancer and their families. This turned out to be more meaningful than I ever imagined it would be, but most of all it was healing to my wounded heart.

When I was considering what the name of the organization should be, I thought back to Tyler's friendship with Daniel and what an impact it had had on all of us. So, I chose "Friendships & Families for Life." It was a small charity, but it reached many lives. I helped the children and the families of the children battling pediatric cancer and other life-threatening illnesses by giving packages of gift cards that could be used for travel. I also helped other like-minded organizations by doing face painting at their fund-raisers. We also help connect these children and families with counseling, financial help, and other resources. I met some amazing people along the way whom I'll never forget. Some of them were children who are no longer with us.

One of these children in particular was Noah. He was one of those incredible children who could light up a room with his smile, his strength, and his charming country accent. I still think of him often, taken from us way too soon. But I know he's walking with Jesus in heaven and he has probably met Daniel by now. My life—and hopefully the lives of others—is better because of the work I did and the people whom I met during the four years my charity lasted. I could tell by the great feelings I had from giving myself and my time, that I was getting more of a blessing in return. You can never outgive God.

Luke 6:38 tells us: *"Give, and it will be given to you. Good measure, pressed down, shaken together, running over, will be put into your lap. For with the measure you use it will be measured back to you."*

Part of the healing process for me was giving back. Once I started helping others, in the way that others had helped me, my cup started to overflow. But remember, you can't give from a cup that isn't already overflowing.

Psalm 103:2–3 instructs us: *"Bless the LORD, O my soul, and forget not all his benefits, who forgives all your iniquity, who heals all your diseases...."* This verse reminds us that not only is the healing of your physical ailments possible, but the healing your spiritual needs is available, as well. David connects the two—iniquities and diseases—and this leads us to "spiritual healing."

Sometimes personal and spiritual healing take longer than we're willing to wait. In John 5:6–8, when Jesus saw a man *"lying there and knew that he had already been there a long time, he said to him, 'Do you want to be healed?' The sick man answered him, 'Sir, I have no one to put me into the pool when the water is stirred up, and while I am going another steps down before me.' Jesus said to him, 'Get up, take up your bed, and walk.'"*

This man had been there for a while and he had tried on many other occasions to get into the healing pool of water. But people kept cutting in front of him, and no one wanted to help. I have often felt like everyone was cutting in front of me in the line, and I have asked many times, when is it my turn? Why doesn't someone help me? Why has God allowed this to happen to me?

Why was the man sick? Did Jesus ask that question? No, He didn't. Although the man could have even been experiencing a self-inflicted illness, Jesus didn't care. Jesus came to help, and the man was healed. Jesus is there for you, too, and trust me, my friends, He can heal your soul.

12
GOD WILL NOT PUT MORE ON YOU THAN YOU CAN HANDLE

I know now that each trial prepares me for the next. Losing someone is never easy, even when you think you're prepared for it. The passing of my father-in-law was no exception. I had lost one dad already, and I wasn't prepared to lose a second one.

I will never forget the phone call my wife received while we were driving to one of Layla's volleyball games. We were halfway to our destination when Elisha's half-sister called and asked us to come over immediately. She wouldn't tell us why or what was wrong, only that something terrible had happened and that we needed to get to her house as soon as possible.

When we arrived, Elisha's sister and stepmother were sitting on the ground in the driveway, their faces in their hands. Elisha parked our car and jumped out.

As soon as she stepped out, her sister stood up and screamed, "He's gone! Dad's gone!" My wife began to sob, asking what had happened.

"He shot himself!"

Elisha began to wail and grabbed on to her sister. At this point, everyone was on their feet crying uncontrollably. I remember thinking that this had to be impossible. Somehow, they had misunderstood, something else had went wrong, and that was why Jim was dead. My wife broke away from her family, doubled over in pain, and began to vomit. The emotional pain had begun to hurt her physically, causing her to become nauseous. And this was only the beginning of the pain of losing him.

This was more than I could bear at this time. All the trials I'd been through had not prepared me for something this shocking. I could not bear this tragedy alone, and neither could I be the rock that my wife and family needed. But Psalm 68:19 tells us, *"Blessed be the Lord, who daily bears us up; God is our salvation."* God is the great Burden-Bearer, and we are to give your burdens to Him to carry. Do this daily; don't wait for it to be too much for you to carry on your own.

So, I did just that. I gave my pain to God because it was more than I could carry myself. I couldn't make sense of any of it. Jim had been a strong, healthy man, with a great sense of humor, someone whom I had come to love like he was my own father. He was always laughing and smiling. He worked hard as a mechanic, owning and operating his own shop. It was just him and his trusty assistant, Mrs. Edna.

Edna was more than an assistant; she was like family. She had worked for Jim twenty years to the day when it happened, and she was the only one there to hear the gunshot come from the back room. She said she had known better than to go in the room, but she kept yelling for him through the closed door. She gave one him one last warning, telling him that if he didn't answer she was going to call 911.

Jim was found dead that afternoon from a self-inflected gunshot wound. Edna was right not to go into that room, as she didn't need to see the aftermath. I know, because I was the only one family member who did go in to see it. No one would come to Jim's garage afterward until the room was cleaned. Edna and I took care of that with the help of a professional cleaning crew. And she and I stayed at the garage for the two days afterward, fielding customers' questions and taking care of the remaining business for the week. It was a difficult couple of days, but she was strong and amazing through it all.

I didn't think the ordeal would bother me as much as it did, but it has been very difficult. It stirred up many bad feelings I had been suppressing for years. The passing of my dad, Tyler's battle with cancer, and being left by my kids and their mother.

There was no foul play found to be involved, and Jim's death was officially ruled a suicide. There had been no real warning signs, other than that morning, he had had a conversation with Edna about God's forgiveness. But it had all happened so fast there was nothing she could have done. She had been a dear friend to Jim, and no one could have asked any more from her than that.

Suicide is a complex issue, and there is no one reason or cause for it. I may never know the real reason why Jim took his own life; we can only speculate on reasons from what we've deduced. I have learned from my own experience that the pain a person feels who is wanting to commit this act, doesn't go away with their passing. It is simply divided up and handed out to all of the family members and friends left behind. If you truly love the people around you, then suicide is not a good answer for your problems. All of his family and friends will carry a part of the pain of Jim's suicide for the rest of our lives.

Whatever was going on with Jim I know could have been handled with help. I believe with all of my heart that having a personal relationship with Jesus, connecting with a strong church family, and surrounding yourself with good people can prevent your self-destruction.

You're not the first person to go through a trial. Even in Bible days, there was no trial that wasn't "common to man," and the same is true today.

I end this book by saying God is faithful, even though humans are not. God will never give up on you. God will not allow a trial to touch your life that He knows that you, together with His help, cannot handle, and He will give you the opportunities and tools that you need to conquer it.

Surviving the Trials by Kenny Dietrich

James 1:12 tells us, *"Blessed is the man who remains steadfast under trial, for when he has stood the test he will receive the crown of life, which God has promised to those who love him."*

EPILOGUE

Writing this book has been such an amazing journey, and I thank you for taking the time to read it. I have learned so much about myself, and it has been much-needed therapy. It has improved my spiritual walk with Jesus and made it stronger. I pray that my testimony has given glory to God and put a smile on your face.

I don't know where life will lead me after this book is completed, but I know that God will show me the way. This has been a leap of faith on my part, and I plan to continue on this path. I know God has great things in store for me and my family. And I know He wants great things for you, too.

If you don't have a personal relationship with God, now is the time. Ask Him into your heart and start your amazing journey with Him. The greatest thing about following Jesus is that you don't have to worry about sin and hell. This doesn't mean you have a free pass to do whatever you want, but if you have a true relationship with Him, you won't *want* to sin again. Sure, we will make mistakes that are not always atrocities, but God understands and will forgive us for these mistakes. It's a change and a way of life that, even during the trials, I promise will be more rewarding than you could ever imagine.

Surviving the Trials by Kenny Dietrich

ABOUT THE AUTHOR

Kenny Dietrich is a practicing wilderness Survivalist & Bushcrafter, Entrepreneur, Philanthropist, and globally recognized YouTuber, but his real trials were as a father, husband, and family man.

In this book he shares his unique experiences and how his faith pulls him through the loss of loved ones, his son surviving cancer and starting over again after hitting rock bottom.

Author's Acknowledgments

Special thanks to:

- My wife, Elisha, for putting up with all of my crazy dreams and ideas
- My mom, Sue
- My children, Tyler, Madison, and Layla
- My brother, Chris, and his girls, Chelsea and Marisa
- All of my friends and extended family members
- St. Jude Children's Research Hospital

www.ingramcontent.com/pod-product-compliance
Lightning Source LLC
Chambersburg PA
CBHW050540300426
44113CB00012B/2203